Advance Praise for *Cold Forge:*

I0186567

Les Brown knows that memory is not necessarily a whole piece. In *Cold Forge*, his second volume of poems set in the North Cove area of the Blue Ridge, he reveals those memories, piece by piece as if reassembling a shattered artifact. The reader encounters an alcoholic father, a long suffering, pious mother, and a difficult life that contrasts with the beauty of the setting. The lore of the family, the farm, and the vibrant characters who inhabit the valley is irresistible. In the end, upon returning, the narrator, though haunted by the ravages of time, is resigned rather than wistful about the place that forged his life.—**Tim Peeler**, author of *West of Mercy*, *Checking Out*, and *First Season*.

In Les Brown's *Cold Forge* "the voices of slaves rise from unmarked graves" mourning the past "to clear way the sorrow." The poet loves "that place of magic long time ago." Memory and imagination make music: the "crickets cry" and "fire flies wink love calls." —**Shelby Stephenson**, poet laureate of North Carolina, 2015-2018. His recent book is *Country*.

In *Cold Forge*, Les Brown welcomes the reader as witness and trusted friend to step into thoughtfully crafted vignettes in verse drawn from personal history, memories, and old family photos. Delving into his Blue Ridge roots in North Carolina, Brown paints the everyday, often harsh realities of hardscrabble people of his boyhood and family farm, and balances the canvas with well-placed brushstrokes of light. Through Brown's artist's eye for detail, the poems in *Cold Forge* quietly but confidently deliver a palpable sense of place, time, and humanity. A masterful storyteller, he breathes life into sympathetic, believable narrators and characters—featuring (or informed by) real people in Brown's circle—achieved with authentic, accessible voice and skillfully woven southern Appalachian dialect-driven dialog. Brown rewards the reader with a beautifully cohesive collection—rich in narrative, vivid in imagery, delightful in form and shape, devoid of sentimentality, and enticing to the senses. *Cold Forge* is memoir in poetry—to be experienced, treasured, and ultimately shared.—**Leslie Rupracht**, *Editor, poet and Author of Splintered Memories*.

Les Brown's *Cold Forge* is an evocative recounting of his life in North Cove in sharp imagery: "broken fences and baked ribs...hidden bourbon and buttermilk...spilled blood and thick molasses." This push and pull of "Juxtapositional" centers his poems in the complex life of a family tied to land and tethered to place. In "Broad Fields and Rushing Water," Brown hinges past and present, "I am still here / and I am still there," bridging time in poems that preserve, remember, and love.—**Alana Dagenhart,** author of *Blood* and *Yellow Leaves.*

Cold Forge

Poems

Les Brown

REDHAWK
PUBLICATIONS

Copyright © 2022 Les Brown

All rights reserved. This book or parts thereof may not be reproduced in any form, stored in any retrieval system, or transmitted in any form by any means—electronic, mechanical, photocopy, recording, or otherwise—without prior written permission of the publisher, except as provided by United States of America copyright law. For permission requests, write to the publisher, at "Attention: Permissions Coordinator," at the address below.

Redhawk Publications
The Catawba Valley Community College Press
2550 UYS Hwy 70 SE
Hickory NC 28602

ISBN: 978-1-952485-72-5

Library of Congress Number: 2022937111

Dedication

To my best editor, critic, and loving wife and poet,
Joyce Compton Brown,
and to my devoted friends who have encouraged my writing.

Acknowledgements

The author gratefully acknowledges the following publications in which these poems, sometimes in a slightly different version. first appeared.

Pinesong: "That Time I Sat on Arthur Dellenger's Tractor"; "Shadows from Lantern Light"   (formerly entitled, "The Barn"); "Backyard Conundrum"
Flying South: "The Wish"; "Aunt Sarah Hula Hoops"
Nexus Poets: "Pause"
Avalon: "Camping in Uncle Dewey's Pasture"
Poetry in Plain Sight: "Winter of 1951"
Kakalak: "Diggy, 1947"; "Sarvis Tree":
Pine Mountain Sand and Gravel: "Painting the Boundary"
Front Porch Review: "Watching the Storm Beyond My Window"
Still the Journal: "Dreams of Flying"
Muddy River Review: "Her Hat"
Black Moon Magazine: "Cold Forge"
Reedy Branch Review: "Cider Barrel"

Table of Contents

I. Childhood

II. The Farm

III. In the Valley

IV. The Return

I'm going out to clean the pasture spring;
I'll only stop to rake the leaves away
(And wait to watch the water clear, I may):
I sha'n't be gone long. -- You come too.

—*Robert Frost*

Childhood

Dreams of Flying

I wanted to fly like the birds—
every child dreams
of cutting gravity's bond—
                    and I did fly
as I ran
down
      the steep
            pasture slope,
leaping skyward on giant steps
above the hoof paths
and close-cropped grass,
feeling the earth
      drop below me.
            If only for a moment,
                    I could touch the clouds.

Time pulled me
down,
                    but I still dream
of leaving earth again,
making loops and spins,
                  looking
                  down
on my small white house,
seeing my tiny father walking
with milk bucket to the barn,
my mother   minute   dashing dishwater
among her
    wilting
        hollyhocks.

I would ride updrafts
like a vulture
searching for the dead
in that gray valley.

The Current

From a photo of our favorite swimming hole featured in Post Magazine, 1958.

We were the same age
when we swam away
hot days in the baptizing pool
of the river,
under the iron bridge
on Pitts Station Road,

a stone's throw
from his house
where his mother
gave us peanut
butter and jelly sandwiches
and iced tea for lunch.

Rickey moved away,
down to town,
to swim in real pools
with girls
while I stayed
in the muddy water

among trout
and horneyhead chubs,
dodging muscle boys who
jumped
from the top girder
of the bridge

while I arched
my arms against
the current
that could sweep
me downstream
toward town.

The Wish

I never had a birthday party
        but Rickey did,
and I was invited. I went
        down the paved road to his house,
a bigger house than ours.
        I took him a dancing man
Daddy made from wood scraps
        he had brought from the factory.

Rickey's house had a bathroom,
        and it was inside
and had a hot water spigot.
        We had a Brownie camera,
but Rickey had a movie projector
        that showed real movies
on a sheet his momma hung
        from the fireplace mantle.

He showed us an Abbot and Costello movie.
        It was funny, especially Costello.
Then we had the fancy cake
        with seven colored candles on it.
Rickey made a wish
        and blew out all of the candles.
I made a wish too.

Stairwell

First high drop of a roller coaster,
 Superman's plunge to save Lois—
  We slid down the banister
   in Grandmother's house,
    over and over when we were small
     and future was nothing
      but a grown-up worthless word.
       It is shorter now,
        dusty in the silent house,
         waiting for our return
          to polish the ancient walnut rail
           as we did while listening to the
            cacophony of kinfolks who left us—
             one by one.

The Pianola

The player piano
rang out ragtime,
"Keep the Home Fires Burning,"
"Are You Lonesome Tonight,"
"Beer Barrel Polka."
I pumped and pumped
and watched the keys
pop up
and down,
phantom music
I could play—
I played and played
as the bellows breath pushed
through the holes in paper rolls.
I could pretend to be my dad,
pretend he didn't breathe his bourbon breath,
but his fingers struck the ivory keys
in perfect time, with a rhythm I never had.

That Time I Sat on Arthur Dellenger's Tractor

Arthur Dellenger's rusting 8N Ford tractor
sat cattycornered near our mail box
where he left it in the mowed hay stubble
of our field when he went home for supper.
Daddy said I was too little to drive.

A short walk down the gravel drive way
was permitted by Momma because
it was the same as going to get the mail.
I went down there and knee-crawled
up on Arthur's padded red seat

that had some stuffing coming out,
pretending to drive like Arthur,
turning the wide black steering wheel
this way and that. The clutch and brake pedals
were out of reach of my short legs, but I pushed

air through my tight lips making tractor sounds,
pulling knobs and pushing buttons. Suddenly
the tractor roared to life, growling like a rabid dog.
It didn't move, but rattled as the motor kept running.
More frantic pushing buttons, pulling knobs

didn't stop the roaring. One knob made the motor
louder. One knob had the letters CHOKE on it.
Pulling that knob as far out as it would go
made the motor start coughing like Daddy did
when he smoked his Camel cigarettes.

It sputtered,
puffed blue smoke,
and died.
Momma asked
why my eyes were red.

Her Hat

Mother wore her broad brimmed straw hat
     in summer's sunshine
when she weeded dahlias,
     irises, snap dragons and zinnias,
taking it off only
     to wipe her sweating brow,
or to savor the sweetness
     of the roses her mother had given her.

When cloud and thunder came
     she hung it
on a nail by the door,
     sat on her front porch,
watching, blessing the freshening rain
     while waiting
for the sun's return.

As days grew short
     and winter came,
silent snow covering bud and leaf,
     bending her to its will
driving her inside, she placed
     her hat on top of the dusty armoire
in her dark cold bedroom.

On the Way Home from the Movies

We went to the movies
        every week
because Daddy didn't want to miss
the next episode of the
        cliff-hanger
short-subject film that ran after the RKO
news reel and Looney Tunes cartoons.
That was before he couldn't miss
        his nighttime bourbon.

He always stopped at Slick Mills'
        service station
        and all-night café
        as we left for home.
My brother and I
always ran inside with him because
        he bought us ice cream cones.
        Momma stayed in the car
holding her purse and lips tight.
        I made my buttered pecan last
        all sixteen miles home.

The Secret

The burnished collie
    waited
beneath the silver maple
for Daddy's
      green Chevy pickup.

I waited
   behind
the boxwood
 to surprise him
    in his old green truck.

Time stood still,
     as Daddy
stepped from behind
    the steering wheel,

reached back
    beneath the seat,
pulled out a flat brown bottle,
    turned it to the blue sky.

***

Mother knew him,
kept the secret
  from me.
I found his cache
  of bottles,
one in the garage toolbox,
one in the hayloft.

***

We watched
as he fell further,
    pleaded,
  yearned to see a change.

I placed his bottle
on our dining table,
     wrote a note,

"Choose, this or me."
He chose the bottle.

               ***

He trudged up a hill
     into a little white church
where he promised
before God—
Nothing changed.

               ***

Mother stayed the course
never acknowledged
the white elephant,
submerged herself
in irises, dahlias
and dishwater.
She would survive
in spite of him.

               ***

I left her alone
with him,
only returning
for duty visits.

               ***

I remember
the gentle father
of my childhood who
went away
into a bourbon world.

Whiskey

I stand on Daddy's shoes
with bare feet.
He walks.
I walk with him,
moving backwards,
clinging,
as he, reeking,
stumbles,
trying to carry me,
my brother,
and my mother
to some better place.

When I step off onto the earth,
turn, walk away,
he recedes,
becoming smaller
and smaller.
I look back
into his weary eyes,
and I walk on,
glancing
over my shoulder.

Target

What are we? Humans? Or animals? Or savages?
What's grownups going to think?
—William Golding

The BB hit me in the back
stinging a small blister
as I ran from the Red Ryder.

The twenty-two-bullet hissed by.
I saw them aim, heard the pop
from far across the grain field
in a pasture among cows.

I was the youngest of the pack.
We all ran free across fields
and mountains. Was I interrupting,
dogging their juvenile freedom?

An old man now, I still ponder
their choices, even when they are dust
by nature's aim and deadly shot.

Camping in Uncle Dewey's Pasture

I carried my blanket, a can of SpaghettiOs
leftover biscuits, salt cured ham
army surplus canteen,
matches and Coleman lantern,
a hatchet and cook kit
up the highway, past family farmland
and ancestral homes.
I met my cousins and friends
in Uncle Dewey's yard
below the Clinchfield Railroad fill.

We climbed the bank, crossed the tracks,
skittered down the other side,
spread barbwire fence,
crawled into close-cropped pasture.
We trudged up the slope near the foot
of steep Honeycutt Mountain
to our level grassy campsite
beside a clear stream in the pasture
where Giardia had yet to reach,
where branch lettuce grew
among green moss and fern.
We built a fire of gathered deadfall
and finished our makeshift meal.

We log-sat in firelight's flicker,
until tales and lies wore thin.
One by one we rose and went
to our peck-order selected spots,
scooped out hip-holes in the turf,
rolled into our warm blankets,
staring at constellations
until their light faded
into dreams of high-finned cars,
hoeing corn, and naked girls.

Winter of 1951

My brown aviator cap was
soft leather lined with rabbit fur.
It had ear flaps that I lowered
when the cold mountain wind
cut through the wool
toboggans my friends wore.

It even had goggles,
made me a man like my uncles
who were flying over Korea.
I pretended to fly and wore it
until the heat of spring
made me raise the flaps,
until the seams wore out,
before I began to see real images
of war through its scratched lenses.

Echoes

The smoke and the fire and the speed, the action and the sound, and everything that goes together, [the steam engine] is the most beautiful machine that we ever made...
—O. Winston Link, American Photographer

I miss those grand steam engines
of the days when I was tall
as half a steel wheel resting on glistening
      rails leading to everywhere.
      I stood on the depot platform watching
white steam puff, puff in slow rhythm
as it waited to be called to duty.
      The shrill whistle spoke, echoes
      respoke from the surrounding hills.

And then the rods began to churn.
      The wheels begin to turn, turn
      turn......turn.....turn...turn..turn turn
in syncopation with surging smoke,
steam roiling from the tall black stack.
Vapor pushing to escape from the massive
boiler chamber began to yield to throttle,
pulling one hundred mystery box cars
      one last time before rusting forever,
      stripped, grown over with vines.

I dreamed of being the engineer
who would wave at wide-eyed kids
from high in my square window.
      They would watch me in awe,
      ruling such massive midnight power.
But dreams of giants die—
Emasculated diesel drove them away
with invisible power hidden beneath
colorful streamlined carapace.
      Grating mechanical voice
      destroyed the vaporous whistle.

Bivouac

Green helicopters
circle once,
land in Uncle Rom's Pasture
among the blackberry briars.
Golden broom straw
whips
at polished boots of soldiers
running
from gale of rotor blades.
Stillness in the valley
is broken by a thrumming beat
as choppers lift off
like dragonflies,
tilt away,
back across Linville Mountain.
Green Berets are practicing
for landing across the sea
in some rice paddy
of some valley
between hills
among other hills.
where water and rice grass
whip
at muddy boots as they slog from
rotor wash
toward high ground
unprotected by lantern light,
warmth
of Uncle Rom's hay loft.

The Farm

Stillhouse Retrospective

The path to the
               falls opens
as we cut and slash our way
through the overgrown trail,
                         unused
since the mountain burned,
                    leaving
charred pine and oak
               in a laced maze.
Catbriers, saplings and laurel
grow thick, where leaves
               had denied them sunlight.
We lop, saw and hack the steep path
until the deadfall ends
               and the air cools,
filled with the scent of wet humus.
We descend to the whisper
of water sheeting over burnished
               flat-fractured rocks,
green with moss
and fern, that step down,
               down, steep
into the churning plunge basin mist.
We tread with care
over wet moss into sunlight,
to the edge of the precipice
               where men with guns
once stood guard,
tended simmering copper-kettled
               sour mash,
sampled the condensed trickle
of clear whiskey, proud of their sweat-
hardened creation, of carrying bushels
               of corn, sacks of sugar, and jugs
beyond all prying eyes.

Under the Sarvis Tree

The serviceberry tree stands strong
beside the pasture fence beyond our barn.
Bees buzz its white blossoms.
Sleeping creatures yawn and stretch,
emerge from beneath winter's cover.

Long ago Methodist Circuit Riders,
delayed by deep snow and winter's freeze,
came to conduct overdue "sarvises"—
a belated wedding, a child's funeral—
to preach rousing sermons
promising liquor-laced sinners new birth.
It was time to till and sow
in the mountain valleys.

I watch pale green leaves
supplant the blossoms, budding
into small green berries hidden
among the foliage, sipping
root-stored food to swell
in the warmth of summer sun,
turning from green to purple-red.

The fruit lures cedar waxwings
to feast as I sit beneath
the branches, scattering
birds devouring the sweet berries
carrying seeds that will survive
their acidic air-born journey,
a chance to be born again.

Lanterns

Spirits in overalls brush by
as I climb the foot-worn ladder
into the loft. The scent of hay
and bourbon lingers, mingles
with voices of men shucking corn.
Wide chestnut boards creak
as dusty children run among shucks
and soft dry hay. Their shadows
from lantern light play on the walls
until they slump in slumber.

The dead drift—they warm the winter,
chill the summer, continuing the tasks
that will never end: sowing, reaping
harvesting, hauling. Their wagon is still
in the wide alley between rows
of stalls sheltering tired wraith mule,
horse, and lean cows that stand still
as blue-white milk pulled from swollen
udders fills hammered tin pails
where cat meows echo in the gloom

Lean-to sheds flanking the barn
droop with age. Square nails lift
from split boards— some spring
from skeletal beams, cling,
fall to earth, one by one.
Tin roof rusts blood that runs,
stains the ashen gray walls.

Cold Forge

Henry's farm shop
stands dark,
velvet-sooty inside
from long use
of the glowing forge
sitting in the center
of the black-packed clay floor
layered with coal dust,
rust, metal chards
from red-hot hammer-forced iron.
Fiery showers sprayed
from foot-pedaled grinder.
A century of sweating hands
shaped mule shoes,
andirons, clevises, and plowshares.
Cold iron festooned its walls
like found art
forged from useless shapes
into solid tools.
Some, strain-broken,
waited to be softened red,
to yield,
renewed by Grandfather's strong muscles.
The ringing of the hammer
on an anvil,
the smell of sulfur
and sweat, still rises
on the hot wind
over dead-stained earth.

Nighttime at the Chicken House

When they flew out of the lot,
over the chicken wire fence
and got in our yard
where they would shit,
I would step in it,
barefoot, squishing
the stinking mush
between my toes,
tracking it into the kitchen,
my mother's sanctuary of cleanliness.

My father and I went
to the chicken house at night,
where the silent chickens crouched,
grasping perch with curved scaly toes.
Round worn Smooth poles
stair-stepped up the back wall
above the row of a dozen
straw-lined nesting boxes
inside the tarpaper covered shack.
With lantern hung from ceiling hook,
he lifted the sleeping chickens
off roosting poles,
held them gently
under his arm
while I cropped each one's long wing feathers
with my mother's heavy pinking shears.

A stealthy skunk sometimes
got into the lot at night,
digging its way under the wire fence,
scenting its way into the chicken house.
The creature would snatch a chicken
off a roosting pole.
The hen would squawk and squawk,
wake up my dad.

He'd grab his shotgun, put on his hat,
stick his bare feet in unlaced shoes,
run to the chicken house, a pale warrior
wearing only droopy drawers—
shoot the skunk.

The stinking dead chicken, unfit
for Sunday dinner, became my duty
to bury deep with no skunk-
warning epitaph.

I buy a carton, a dozen extra-large
Eggland's Best from Food Lion,
eggs that never rested in warm straw
nest under mother hens,
each egg from an identical Leghorn,
one white chicken among thousands
caged in long, arched buildings,
standing on steel, not knowing
of low fences to challenge flight,
imprisoned, safe from murderous skunk.

Cider Barrel

Cider of sweet apples
ground by cog
and press of cider mill
ferments, beckons
men and sneaking kids
by twist of barrel tap,
to taste the bubbling juice
as it changes
toward its inevitable
vinegar end.

They sip and drink
the sour wine,
same as the Egyptians
of pharaoh's time,
ignoring the myriad
writhing vinegar
eels in the cloudy
golden liquid
along its journey
to pickle jar,
vinegar pie,
and cult-avowed
miracle cures.

Juxtapositional

Allis Chalmers tractors and crocheted lace
       Fat hogs and lattice-topped apple pie
Turned black earth and soft feather beds
       Sprouting corn and rambling farmhouse
Flood water and baptizing on Sunday
       Manured stalls, and cold spring water
Broken fences and baked ribs
       Bickering kin and glowing forge
Quivering guts and sweet-smelling soap
       Chopped wood and Christmas gifts
Factory tired fathers and perking coffee
       Shotguns and Easter eggs
Hidden bourbon and buttermilk
       Inexorable time and aproned grandmother
Spilled blood and thick molasses
       Dry hay and wet newborns
Dying grandfather and broken land
       Tombstones and television.

In the Valley

Uncle Henry

Dad's Uncle Henry pocket knife lay in a drawer
filled with the remnants of his life.
His father had given it to him
when he was eight years old,
told him it would last
a lifetime. He carried
it everywhere.

He used it to clean under his
nails as he sat on the back
pew at church, not listening.
He honed the knife blades
every day, honed
and honed until
the blade passed
his test of shaving
his forearm.
The blades
grew small,
thin and
narrow.

He used his Uncle Henry to cut corn,
peel apples, cut bailing twine,
whittle gewgaws for his kids
and a windmill for the hog lot
fence post, just to watch it
turn, pointing, pointing
to where
he would
never go.

Before the Lines

There is a crack in everything, that's how the light gets in.
—Leonard Cohen

The flashlight sitting deep on a closet shelf
belonged to my father. It was his and his alone.
      He used it to light his way
      to the barn before sunrise,
      to see in plank-crack dimness,
      the place he had hidden his whiskey,
      to milk our brindled cow

He used it when lightning struck at night,
      to search for match and lamp
      to dim-light our house
      the way he had before
      the linés were hung.
      He said, "Leave it alone.

So I'll know where it is to keep you safe."
And then he died. I heard his words
      each time I saw the flashlight
      that no one would touch,
      even when it sat
      corroded in a pool of acid.

Hanging by the Door

Cock your hat – angles are attitudes.
—Frank Sinatra

That felt fedora, stained
brown as garden mulch
hung on a nail beside the kitchen door.
Its brim and band defined him,
a farmer driven from the divided land
into a dreary windowless factory,
thirty-five years worn, tired,
wilted, with drooping shoulders.

He wore it as he stripped fodder,
milked the cow, and cut firewood.
He wore it at his small desk
in the corner of a factory stock room.
Beneath the hat, his weary mind was
filled with debt, duty, doubt, and icy love.
Still, with a bourbon toast, he could
don his hat, cock it aslant, pretend
to have a certain air of *savoir faire*.
It still hangs by the door, his
sweat-stains in the band.

Watching the Storm Beyond the Window

Outside my window a hammered
steel sky cries through thunderous
blows where brilliant tendrils light
wetting leaves. Roots drink rain shaken
from the anvil of heaven, violent
stars shine above in the forge of space.

How thin my window of refuge
against such power unfolding
where fragile flowers bloom,
babies nurse at mothers' breasts,
where lace-veined butterfly wings
will spread delicate from chrysalises.

Whirligig

The wooden Dutch woman
shakes, loose-jointed,
as she swings a compass path
churning, churning, churning.
turning.in the slightest breeze.
Propeller and cam move her arms
up and down in unending rhythm
where she labors, sentinel
over summer's withered crops.
My father shaped her aproned skirt,
her bonnet, wooden shoes,
and broad-thin wind vane
from scraps of bed, dresser—
ivory maple he brought home
from his job before the fall.
He jig-sawed her shape,
hinged her arms, and waist,
painted her bright-tulip
red and green,
whittled and sanded
a propeller, joined
it to her mittened hands
with coat hanger wire—
now rusted. Her eyes
looked toward his silent shop
with every passing breeze.

Diggy, 1947

For my grandmother, Mary Jane (Diggy) Brown,

She wore a flour covered apron
over her long dress with tiny blue
and pink flowers, hint of those she grew
in her garden: larkspurs, poppies, hollyhocks,
where she was seen so often digging
among her myriad of colors.
That's why we called her Diggy.

Her black, deep-set eyes sparkled,
accented her soft round face. Laced tight
hair pulled into one long gray braid
fell below her waist. I remember
a splay of wrinkles flaring at corners
of her sunken mouth, her guttural laugh
that arose from deep within.

In my yellowed photo stored as digits
she is holding a pail beneath spout
of well pump, where she brought
the knife to cut red-ripe watermelons
and stirred her thick custard made
for young boys to crank in the White Mountain
ice cream churn on summer evenings.

She is now my Windows wallpaper,
behind icons, before smokehouse
and chicken lot, at the well,
holding, pressing pump handle,
still watching for water's rise,
to flow down my screen, old grief
that cannot be saved to cloud.

Aunt Sarah Hula Hoops

She's swinging her hips in circles,
  keeps the Hula Hoop riding in orbits.
    Her short gray hair shines in noon sun,
      bright as the smile on her wrinkled round face.
    Her floured apron wafts in the breeze.
  She has no reason for joy.
Her father had beaten out
    her unborn passion child.
      Still, she shall not bend to his will
        on the crumb of land thrown to her
        like a scrap from his laden table.
      She laughs, and sips family bourbon,
    keeps the rhythm of life moving
above the earth in which he lies.

Back Yard Conundrum

Moles with their fossorial feet, tiny eyes,
      down-soft fur, and piggy nose
           have tunneled
around my raised bed garden
      beneath wiry Bermuda sod,
on into my lawn, raising a maze
      of soft writhing ridges,
occupants unseen by cat and hawk.
      They dig and dine in darkness.
Worm and grub fear their
      sharp teeth and super sense of smell.
My mother stood watch in our garden,
      statue still—
with hoe in hand, looking
      for heaving earth
where a mole may make way
      among her vegetable roots,
rip them in search of grub and worm
      aerating earth, loosening soil,
helping vegetables grow,
      destroying others—
until arching arm and blade swung down,
      ending the conundrum.
I will allow the moles in my yard to run
      beneath my feet, increase their maze,
annoy my neighbor's sense of aesthetic lawn,
      to find the pests that chew flower and fruit.
I stand, watch the earth
      at tunnel's end for motion,
think of the creatures living below.
      Content, I walk away, leave them safe
          from talon, claw and hoe.

Release

The dam of the fishing lake broke
below their house on Mackey Road

at the same time Grandmother died,
taking her Holy Spirit back Home.

All of the fish were flushed down
to the river, a greater, safer place

where no lines with hooks and lures
dangled daily, where temptation ceased

and there was shelter.
She lay in her coffin while we sang,

"Shall We Gather at the River."
The lake-bed filled with silt.

Weeds and trees have grown
along the bank of the brook

A deep-cut fish adorns her gravestone.
where the creek flows on.

Just one Camel

I caught Momma smoking
    there in front of her cookstove,
strait-laced daughter
    of a Godly Baptist woman
who obeyed every commandment
    and added a few:
thou shalt not smoke,
    thou shalt not drink,
thou shalt not fornicate.

Momma's world-wise sister,
    Mary, put her up to it,
gave her one of her Camels—
    only one, never another.
When Momma saw me watching her
    sinning right there in her kitchen,
she opened the eye of the stove
    and threw that Camel right into
the fire and brimstone.

Abandoned Graves

You may choose to look the other way
but you can never say again that you did not know.
—William Wilberforce

What purpose the tall stone
over the Confederate bones

slave owner, miller and distiller?
He rode his white stallion into
family legend and celebrity,
into stories that had grown
in bourbon-laced brain and word,
until that nineteen-year-old
boy became the image of Lee,
his coat dripping with medallions.

The stone stands in briars, weeds
and saplings, gathering moss,
eroding. His name fades with
his legend, now stained like
the bleeding oxide on his stone.
He lies alone with his wife,
his father in the Home Guard—
all silent, as the voices of slaves
rise from unmarked graves.

Sitting for a Photo, 1918

John Madison Hensley and his wife
        sit on frayed ladder-back chairs
before a steep field of mixed
        aging cornstalks and brambles.
He's holding crutches, arms tense
        in an old wrinkled dress coat,
his deep-set eyes
        dark beneath a bald crown.
White beard drapes to his chest,
        long and thick, a thing of pride.
Mary is seated beside him,
        knees clasped, touching his thigh.
She is wearing her black Sunday dress
        with high tight collar, and long hem.
Her leathery face is weathered
        with strained narrow eyes,
high cheeks and arched lips sunken, toothless.
        Her graying hair twists into a bun.
She clutches a tiny bouquet of daisies
        in her left hand, like those growing at their feet.
They touch her husband's arm.

Photo of Great Grandmother Mary Hall Hensley

The brindled cow is hers.
A puckered smile
of her toothless mouth
can be seen within
the shadow of her
bonnet. She stands
relaxed in her long
sack-cloth dress
and high-topped shoes
before a lean-to shed.
She rests a hand
on her heifer while John
is there at his duties
in the distance.

Turning the Pages

Her shining dark-brown hair
is still there in her photos taped
into the frayed album, it caught
my father's eye at that dance,
long before he lost his way.

I remember it
curling around her face
as she brushed it behind her ear
and re-secured it with bobby pins,
sweating over the pressure cooker
filled with jars of green beans
or leaning on her hoe as she rested
from tending her dahlias and irises.

The pages of the album
mark years of my indifference,
avoiding my staggering father.
Later, on duty visits, I'd find
her silvery-blue hair tightly curled
by the lady in the rest home salon,
smelling of chemicals as I pressed
my lips into its thin stiffness.

The Return

The Encounter

The house had been painted green
in some distant past. Now the porch
sags, its tin roof rusting.
Three skinny cats loll
on and old sofa with stuffing
erupting from its seams.
A long-boned red dog sniffs
my feet while I stand in the bare yard
before the old man—a living scarecrow,
thin faced, hooked nose,
watery eyes close set, alert.
He's wearing thread-bare overalls
over his grayed long johns.

"You might have known my Dad,"
I say. *"He was Gene Brown.*
We bought the Stillhouse
land from my cousins."
I point up the mountain
behind his house.
"Oh yeah, I knowed him,
Gene Brown. We used to
make a little, sell a little,
drink a little—You want
somethin' to drink?"

He's as much a part of this place
as the clear water he uses to make
his moonshine somewhere upstream
among the collapsed boulders.

Homecoming

I returned to the vacant
plot—charred, scattered with chards
of white asbestos.
It is only an ethereal gap
filled with no substance.
I did not see the rising smoke,
the licking flames,
did not feel the heat,
did not smell the past
as it vaporized, taking
kitchen, bedrooms,
dining room, front room,
melting the picture window,
and collapsing Mother's front porch
where she sat
watching her hummingbirds.
I did not hear the cracking,
see the crumbling
of the asbestos siding
my father had added with pride.
before he lost his job.

Painting the Boundary

I climb the ridge, hack my way
through cat briar, poison ivy,
deadfall and muscled laurel limbs,
searching trunks of pine and oak
for healed slash marks and stain
in age-old boundary trees.
I refresh the survey marks
with bright-red paint dividing
no one's land into yours and mine.
I'll be proud that mine is mine
though I know it's all its own
in spite of paint and axe.

Clearing the Lot

Two fallen hemlocks,
      victims of adelgid and western
wind, lie where my home stood,
      where I took my first breath
in a January mountain chill.
      Kudzu rises into the trees.
Sweet scent of wisteria hangs
      in the spring air, its muscled
vines gripping the last dying
      white pine my father had planted
beside the two-track driveway
      to serve as a wind-break,

offer shade from southern sun.
      Scattered lilies-of-the valley,
and daffodils are the only flowers
      left from my mother's garden,
what's left of her pride. She was duty
      bound—cooking, canning, washing
clothes, cleaning the small house
      that stood on the lot while my father
worked at his factory job.
      At the edge of the lot is a forest,
a swale marking the path
      beside the barbed wire fence

where my collie, Pard, and I
      drove the cow home for milking.
Short stubs of rusted wire
      protrude from deep within trees.
The house burned, barn decayed,
      father, mother, brother gone,
I have returned not to bring
      back the dead, but to savor the view
of the broad farm valley,
      the old homes, the mountains,
to clear away the sorrow.

A Summer Saturday at the Orchard

Go between the shelves
of apple butter, chowchow,
elderberry jam, pickled okra,—
past the ice cream counter
and tip jar—
to the Bluegrass beat
of base fiddle, mandolin,
five string banjo and guitar,
to the clacking, tapping,
shuffling feet.

Coiffed women
with blue hair spin
under raised arms
of their silvered men.
A bent woman shuffles,
balancing on her walking cane,
joins the beat.
A young boy clogs
with awkward intensity
before his dancing teacher.

Florida, Georgia, Tennessee tags
join the Carolina cars
in the lot
of the Orchard at Altapass
where apple trees are only an excuse,
a vestige of the past,
a drawing card for tourists
and cool-altitude,
mountain residents,
the native,

the northern and southern transplants,
retired,
searching for rest
and finding joy in sweating
on the vibrating plywood floor
in rhythm,
forming a common bond
of disparity
within layered Blue Ridge
undulations.

Broad Fields and Rushing Water

I am the youngest.
I watched
as the last of the boys of the land,
hearty but old
died of the insidious unseen enemy of 2020.
His pristine home,
several outbuildings,
groomed lawn and tended fields
are now still.
A great pine has fallen across his meadow.

I am still here
and I am still there, alone.
I have watched them
like old photographs fading,
until the image cannot be seen.
My tether was never broken—
It held me to that place,
the land, the water, the forest,
and the few that were left—
and then another
and another and another
were laid to rest.

A rock church built by our grandfathers
was our anchor,
the graveyard beside it
a reminder of ticking time,
of the inevitable known
but denied in our youth.
We broke free of chrysalises
into adulthood,
into new worlds.
Some remained,
most flew away
only to return as old men
restoring past memories,
bringing their children
to savor that place
when time stopped in summers.

We were cousins
connected by land and blood
roaming the forests,
camping by clear streams, swimming,
hoeing corn,
helping our tired fathers with harvest
hoping for miracles.

There is a place of broad fields
and rushing water
where young boys insentiently
celebrated life unbound.

About the Author

Les Brown attended Appalachian State University and the University of Southern Mississippi and is professor emeritus at Gardner-Webb University. He has published poetry and short stories in several journals, including Pinesong, Kakalak, Streetlight Magazine, Pine Mountain Sand and Gravel, Main Street Rag, and Still the Journal. He is also a potter, and visual artist whose work has been featured in regional journals such as Moonshine Review and Broad River Review. Two of Les's poems were nominated for the 2020 Pushcart Prize by the North Carolina Poetry Society. Les lives in Troutman, NC. His poetry book, "A Place Where Trees Had Names," was published by Redhawk Publications, 2020.

www.ingramcontent.com/pod-product-compliance
Lightning Source LLC
Chambersburg PA
CBHW071241090426
42736CB00014B/3178